The

"Keep on Going" Spirit

by Ted Lewis

The
"Keep on Going"
Spirit

by Ted Lewis

Business Management Consultants Company
Kettle Falls, Washington

For information, address:
Keep Going Publishers
Box 545 Kettle Falls, WA 99141

ISBN#: 0-9661682-0-8
Library of Congress Catalog Card Number
97-77673

Second Printing, 1999

Cover Design by Christopher Thorsen

Printed by Cascade Graphics
Wenatchee, Washington
United States of America

Paleolithic Lamp

This book is dedicated to my mother and father.

Foreward

While Ted Lewis asks us to think, this book is not an intellectual exercise. It is an affair of the heart, mind, and soul. His talks are not something you get, they are something you become. You know it in your bones. Your bones may know it before your mind does.

He sees who we are and how we may live with each other. He is the person who has hope for all of us because he believes we can change our behavior. We can change our lives. We can be ourselves. It can be done. Lewis tells precisely how to begin.

He speaks of things most of us sweep under the carpet at 4:00 A. M. on sleepless nights. He speaks so candidly and directly of love that he bears his soul, he is vulnerable. Most of us are embarrassed by such frankness as the risks for speaking intimately are terribly high. Perhaps his courage may encourage us to reconsider the decision to remain silent.

The conceptual leaps occur with

deceptive ease as though he is seeing many layers at once. The author's insight is so piercing that he allows us to catch sight of the nature of things. Normally solid concepts become translucent and we can see into them, if only momentarily, and glimpse the structure of how they fit together.

Reading Lewis is like a tour through fascinating new terrain. His words seem to foster a climate of receptive wonderment. One finds oneself utterly engaged.

The "Keep On Going" Spirit is a collection of unrehearsed talks, reflections, and ideas of the author. He has been edited as little as possible to retain the original spontaneity. Masculine pronouns and words such as *mankind* have been preserved to reflect natural speech. The author's thoughts are always inclusive of women. Repetition is inevitable when ideas are being formulated in an impromptu way. The grammar, correct or incorrect, has been retained as spoken since each phrase is like a brush stroke showing the evolution of ideas.

The Editors

Preface

Before we can talk about anything, we have to have a meal in our stomachs and know that the next meal is coming.

Hopefully, we have an annual assurance of what we're going to eat.

Then we have a brief moment where, with your permission, we can consider being civilized and what being civilized means.

Contents

Love Becomes
The Norm

With your permission, please consider that every day, through every day and sometimes through the night we consider, we wonder who and what we are and why we do the things we do and why we don't do many of the things we may have done.

Each individual needs the balance, the stability of knowing that we are continuously loved, appreciated, and a love that doesn't require from us a form of proof—a love that we can expect so it is unnecessary to attain some particular standard that makes us worthy.

We are loved because of what and who we are not because of what and who we may be or may become. Love needs to be regarded as a

constant. It doesn't change. It doesn't
deviate. It's based on trust, mutual
respect, self-respect, and a glimpse, a
series of glimpses into all these things
that make up the magnificence of each
and every human being.

It is meaningful to allow
ourselves, permit ourselves to recognize
that all of us are beings who are as
significant and as perfect as every leaf,
every rock, every grain of sand, every
drop of water, every cloud. As we begin
to see, allow ourselves to see the
vastness of each individual, then love
becomes the norm.

Fear is lessened. Fear is
diminished. Fear is not all-absorbing.
Fear is not tainting our enjoyment of
the beauty that surrounds us, beauty
that is in us, in all of us. This does not
mean that you will not meet people that
you're not too crazy about. But because
you are not too fond of a person, this
does not give license to injure, to hurt,
to harm, or to ignore. Whenever we
view another, we view mankind in the
light of what he is and what she is,
we're viewing magnificence. Whether
it's visible or not, the magnificence is

there.

Mankind is all meaning. Mankind is what this world and universe is all about. Each of us is a part of this. Each of us is connected, each of us can see if we wish, that the most common thing, the common, the constant, the most ordinary thing that we have is perfection. Yet we act as though it is impossible, exclusive, unusual. Yet every cloud you see is a perfect cloud. Every leaf on every tree is a perfect leaf. Every grain of sand is perfect. So is every rock. The stars, moon, sun, everything is perfection. We deny ourselves. We negate ourselves when we consider that we are less or we have the illusion that we are more. There isn't anyone more than anybody. We have all these things. We are all these things. And this is what we need to look at, enjoy, admire.

Communication

*I*n order to communicate in light, I must ask again for your permission. I believe it is meaningful to understand that everything you do is important. You are a single, original, unique individual. You cannot be more than another person. They cannot be more than you. You are the only one of you, yet all *yous* are in a sense equal. But not the same.

Today, mankind has mass communication, literacy, high tech, pictures, and information, and yet one of our greatest difficulties we have is communicating with each other. I mean when I say communication, that when I say something, you know what I have said and I know what you have said by your reply, or acknowledgement, or disagreement.

We need to communicate almost to the point of absurdity. We need to strive for communication so that it seems on the surface ridiculous. In other words: I know that you know that I know that you know what I have said. The same thing is true when you have spoken.

Now we have the difficulty of terminology. We have the difficulty of language. We have the difficulty of the evolution of words or the decay of generations of words. Words change. Our attitude toward words changes. So communication is vital in order for us to live together on this earth. We need to recognize each other and through this recognition of each other we have a basic platform, we have a basic foundation, a mutual and basic foundation for understanding each other regardless of race, color, intelligence, culture, or distance between our various countries.

In other words, we need to have the mutuality of an organization, an association; the mutuality of each other, the recognition through and with communication that we are all members of the human race, all of us. We all have a connection with each other. We all recognize each other as fellow human beings. We all belong to the same club, whether you are a girl scout, a boy scout, a biker, a salesman, a policeman—whatever the walk of life. We need to recognize and see that we have a chance, we have the opportunity, we have the ability to talk because we all mutually agree on one thing. The one thing we can mutually agree on is how we feel individually and that that feeling be respected by all other individuals; and that other individuals, their feelings be respected, acknowledged. Their feelings appreciated without malice.

All great thinkers throughout the ages, all countries, all cultures, many centuries, many languages, the great thinkers from India, China, Egypt, Mohammed, Buddha, Confucius, Christ, Moses, many many throughout the ages have said a very similar thing which we refer to as "Do unto others as you would have others do unto you." Now this seems always overly simplistic and in a way, nebulous, but I think when we consider, "Do unto others as you would have others do unto you," I think it needs to be broadened a bit so that we can see: you cannot care for another or exhibit your understanding, love, appreciation without self-respect. If you do not have or you do not allow your own magnificence to be understood and accepted by yourself, it makes it extremely difficult to care for another, or to "do unto others."

So, for the clarity in communication, for clarity and the ability to speak with one another—regardless of language, creed, color, race—regardless, we need to have an acceptance, a simple acceptance that allows us to be a member of this world with a sense of appreciating, seeing the wonder that is mankind.

Through this vision which has been repeated and given to us by many, many people, it is time we recognize the value, the significance of caring, of having an interest, a vital interest; and knowing that everything we do is important, is significant and that there isn't any one person who is more than another and there isn't a person who is less than another.

We do not have magnificence through achievement and through striving. We can attain and strive for many things but each human's magnificence has been given to him or her at birth. It's not something that we have the ability to earn or achieve. This recognition of each other is an equality but it isn't an equality based upon arrogance or pride, or a sense of power, but rather a simple understanding that if you could see every person, every person in the world, if you could see them at the age of three you could not help, you could not restrain, you could not stop or keep from loving them in all their wonderment.

We have on this earth many examples, many examples of perfection. We have perfect snowflakes by the millions and the trillions; and perfect clouds by the billions, and perfect grains of sand and perfect leaves and perfect trees and perfect drops of water and perfect mountains. We need to see this magnificence that has been given to us even though it is obvious we have closed our eyes to perfection, magnificence, and intelligence for too long.

Mankind is worthy. All mankind is worthy. And through our worthiness we can know the meaning of life and then because we can know and understand each other, many of our vast problems which seem to be insoluble because they have lasted for thousands of years can be solved. The balance can be restored. People can enjoy life. We can all see in light.

Depression

Especially for this chapter I need your permission to state that all of us at particular times in our lives have feelings of depression, frustration, anger. We do not understand really why these feelings of depression seem continuous, seem to occur often. It seems as though a lot of our thinking time or reflecting time is taken up by these feelings that things aren't really so hot, "I don't feel so great, I really don't know why these feelings of unhappiness continue."

Many of our feelings of depression, discomfort, our limited sense of well-being are caused from fear. Fear that we're not worthy may be very old. I think it usually is. It may come from our childhood when we didn't understand a lot of things we were told so they seemed to us at the time to be rejection or you're not doing so well; you're not really a very good person.

Now these things when we're young are very easily misunderstood. There are so many things that we need to learn at this time and because our emotions are dominant when we are young, our intellectual, logical feelings haven't moved over as it were into something where our feelings are minimized and we develop more of a thinking, considering, reflecting process.

When we were young, we reacted naturally first of all while we were learning about thinking. As we continue through life and we continue to total up the score each day, each year of how we are doing and we have many concepts of what we think success is and what we think failure is and we all have a different version of what constitutes failure—our thinking seems to become a form of unsatisfactory bookkeeping.

When we consider success or failure oftentimes both of these things are bothersome. We may fear failure or we may fear success. Success may bring on more responsibilites, greater effort on our part, more expectations of us that we don't think we want to go through because we don't think we want to cope with it. The sense of failure can be exceedingly harsh because usually our own self-judgments are the most demanding and I think the most damaging. We must consider that all descriptions of success and failure are limited.

We have a great force known as public opinion. Public opinion, which consists of friends, neighbors, relatives, people we work with—that's usually our public opinion standard; unless we're politicians, celebrities, people who have vast audiences and their public opinion is much more abstract.

Now, the opinions of our worth are up to us. There are a few basic things that are significant to all of us: how we treat each other, what kind of respect do we have for ourselves? The respect that we have for ourselves is not based upon how much money we have in the bank, or what kind of car we drive. Do we live at an address that is very exclusive? It is none of these things. It is how we feel about ourselves in regard to others and what we do that we regard as satisfying.

One of the things that allows depression to continue is a rather ridiculous statement that is quite common today, "Don't get mad, get even." Now when things happen to you that depress you and frustrate you and concern you and

it is in direct regard to other people—
they do something that you believe is
harmful to you, annoying to you. So
you're going to do something to them to
so-called 'even the score'—this is
ridiculous and all you're doing is
continuing the self-destruction,
depression, grief, the agony, the anger
and nothing is accomplished, nothing is
meaningful.

You cannot have great satisfactions
from revenge, vengeance, putting down
another person, a triumphal feeling:
"Well boy, I sure showed that guy. I
straightened him out." This is childish. It
does not lead to a civilized person. No
matter how intense your anger may be.
No matter how your sense of fair play is
affronted. No matter how much injustice
you perceive in a situation where some
things are holding you back, annoying
you, causing you discomfort.

We hurt people, many people, often
through our own indifference, our
ignorance, our blindness. We do this. This
does not mean, therefore, because we do
this, you've done this too often therefore
you're now a terrible person. No, what it
means is you're not using your
awareness, your senses and reacting to

people as they are. You can't see people in a judgmental sense. You can't see people in a labelled sense. You can't put something on them and say this person is this and that sticks.

To know another person and what their circumstances are is exceedingly difficult. This is very far-fetched. We need to constantly be aware of reacting to them with all of our feelings of goodness and recognizing in them that despite what a pain they can be, that there is a lot more to that person than what is apparent on the surface or in their actions. You need to understand and accept that the only things in life that are good and meaningful are brought to us through our knowledge and intelligence, our understanding, our thoughts, our compassion; and ignorance, stupidity, blindness, and indifference is not the way to see your fellow man and particularly yourself.

Every Child Is Your Child

Your permission is again requested. We can know and get along with all of our fellow man and one of the ways in which we realize that this can occur is through our children. Raising, rearing, taking care of a child is one of the most demanding tasks that mankind can perform. It is also inconvenient, difficult, and yet one of the most satisfying of all of our endeavors.

A child learns in the beginning because it has trust and faith even though it may not know what these words may mean. The child has trust and faith in parents, people around it, relatives, those who care for it and are interested in this child's well being. To raise a child, we need to teach, to explain as best we can. When the child is very young, he or she does not understand many words. Even at a very early age we need to show the child, demonstrate, help it to make decisions.

The parent makes decisions for a child as, for example, when you're holding the child and you're on the telephone and the child tries very hard to eat the telephone, that is not what it needs to eat. The child, in the beginning, is not able to make decisions that are correct. Whatever a child can reach, be it something dirty or a handful of oatmeal, it will try to put it in its mouth and see if it isn't something tasty. The child is what we, in the beginning, make of it, through our influences, our stability, our care, our affection, our attention. And the child is a twenty-four-hour-a-day, seven-day-a-week task for its parents.

A child is not something that we can just have like perhaps a pet. It requires our fullest attention. The child needs to know constantly even if you're not doing anything with it at a particular moment, it needs to know that you're present, you're around, you're close by so if it has some difficulty it can holler and yell and know that it will get immediate attention. As

the child gets older, many times the
child wants to do things on its own and
it will. But even though it does much of
its investigation, its learning, its
examination by itself, it still needs to
know that adults, its parents, relatives,
neighbors, friends, the people who are
helping to care for this child are always
available. In my experience, it does not
appear that there can be too many
people involved in caring for any child.

The child is faced with many
things to learn and if we present too
many things for the child too quickly, it
may lose interest in learning. And often
children lose interest in learning from
others at an early age. When we are
raising a child we do not need to
consider that the child in some way has
to prove to us or prove to itself in a form
of demonstration that it is okay through
its achievements, its grades in school,
whatever the criteria at a particular age.

A child is loved and cared for
whether it demonstrates some great
capabilities or not. If the child has to
consider that love needs to be earned
and approval needs to be earned by its
accomplishments, we're giving the child
a burden that may be too great. A child

does not have to earn love. I do not believe love can be earned. Approval—yes.

We can express approval at times but while the child is investigating, while it is doing experiments, while it is learning there are many things it will do that may be shocking and really don't meet with your approval. But the child needs to know that the child is still okay in your eyes even when you do not approve of a particular action or conduct at a given moment.

A child needs to see through its most powerful influences, the parents, what the world in general is all about—whatever that world may consist of: the home, the neighborhood, downtown, shopping centers, wherever. The child needs to see how to conduct itself by what the parents do, how they respond, how they handle situations.

A child is one of the most meaningful things in our entire lives and when we see and understand the beauty, the fascination, the magnificence of a child, it is not so difficult then to see the magnificence of our fellow human being. Every child is your child in a sense. In our minds and in our hearts we know that this is true.

What We Are

May I have your permission to say that no one is more than me. No one is less than me. No one is the same as me.

When we look at each other and we consider ourselves and what we are, there is no room for division. We are all connected. Everything we do is important and all of us have meaning. We do not have to achieve this meaning. We do not have to strive for it. It is given. We all know. We all have the awareness to understand and accept each other for what we are: another human being.

Throughout our lives we do not hurt another. We do not cause injury that can be brought about by a look, a word, a phrase, an expression, or physical harm. These are things that will not permit us to be regarded as civilized human beings.

We have many civilizing

institutions. We strive for contentment, peace with each other.

The answers to all our difficulties are old ones. They've been ever-present. There are no difficult answers. Most of our considerations and concepts are based upon the strongest of all of our feelings—our desires and wants. We really only need a few things. We need food, shelter, and the company of loved ones. This is not something that requires great striving, great endeavor, a strong effort to achieve. As long as we can go through a twenty-four hour period knowing that we have not harmed and not hurt another, that is an achievement in itself.

When we look at what's been going on throughout the ages we are aware of the so-called rise and fall of civilizations and we never really understand why they fell. We don't understand why civilization isn't more of an ongoing thing. I believe that it isn't, because we don't start with ourselves and each other. Civilization has a tough road. We cannot know love unless we respect each other and ourselves. We cannot love another, we cannot enjoy another, we cannot really be with another unless we do not harm each other.

Love is not earned. It is not achieved. Love is something we all have, we all may enjoy. And we do not have to strive or look for it. When we consider the value of each person which is without limit; when we consider all the things that we've been given—our senses, our intellect, our awareness—it does not matter who appears to be the strongest, the most powerful, the richest, or the wisest.

We all have these things. We are all capable. All of us have a beauty and magnificence that is not hidden. You need to allow yourself to look. This is why I say, *No one is more, no one is less, no one is the same. We are all unique.*

We have the same needs, we have similar needs. We have the ability to enjoy, not to enjoy as being a goal or an achievement. We call it the pursuit of happiness. I don't think happiness needs to be pursued. It needs to be accepted and the only way it can be accepted is knowing that each man, each person, each woman, each child, regardless of ethnic background, culture, color, religion, or attitude is okay. It's not a matter of judgment. It's not a matter of a decision. This is the constant changing of all the beauty around us and all this needs to be a knowing, not an act of faith, not a feeling or belief; not something that can say maybe but rather *it is, we are, they are* and *we always will be.* We always may know, if we choose, we all may enjoy. We all may have the privilege of recognizing each other. It is our responsibility.

Everything that mankind has ever wanted or desired is here. Because it may be overlooked through our indifference, inertia, does not mean it doesn't exist. We can close our eyes and say it isn't happening. We can be preoccupied with all the many things that we do, that we feel are very necessary and yet so many of them are not.

We need food, shelter, the company of loved ones. We need to know constantly that we are all right, that we are acceptable because we do not harm, we do not hurt, we enjoy, and appreciate. We do not judge, we do not condemn ourselves or others. We are human beings who are learning, just beginning to learn and use our intelligence, our feelings of goodness, completeness, and joy. We are in many ways like small children, small children who can still see life as a total, complete, constant enjoyment.

Ugly Thoughts

*Y*ou may not wish to give your permission for this chapter.

Many of us, during the course of a day, have thoughts, feelings, that come to us apparently without any reason. Many of these thoughts cause us considerable discomfort, wonderment. They puzzle us because they seem grotesque, unreal, ugly thoughts that are unpleasant. They may be thoughts of violence, sexual; they may appear to us pornographic. They may be thoughts that are confusing because of their ugliness.

They seem to be inappropriate to our daily lives, to our enjoyment, to our work, to our satisfactions, getting along with others. They seem to us to be unusual and yet they persist. We have these thoughts often during the day. We wonder, for days, weeks, months, years, throughout our lifetime actually, and we wonder and wonder if there is something about us that isn't all right. Perhaps we're not worthwhile. Our feelings seem so ugly perhaps because we imagine we're not really worthy people.

Everyone has these thoughts. Everyone. Whether they speak of them or tell anybody about them, they still have them. We all have them because our senses, our hearing, seeing, sense of smell, taste, touch, all these senses are always recording, constantly recording twenty-four hours a day, recording all the experiences that we see, feel, all our sensual experiences since birth, perhaps prior to birth.

Because so many things come to us sometimes in great quantities and our senses are recording all of this information that we get as we go through life, in every phase of life, we are deluged at times, surrounded. It's constant, even though we may not be aware of any particular thoughts, feelings, impressions, sensations in any kind of order or any kind of way that we can sort out, it's all recorded. Whether we want it to be or not, it is recorded in our minds. So when we are exposed to—what friends tell us, what we get from books, radio, newspapers, magazines—whatever the source of the entertainments—we absorb all this information whether we're actively aware of it or not. Because we do, it is oftentimes played back to us in our thoughts in a disjointed, scattered, or fragmented way.

So this occurs. We do not need to dwell on or consider or continue to consider thoughts we may regard as shameful or guilty. The guilt and shame really don't have much significance or meaning. Our actions and what we do and think is what we are. As long as we're considering in life, with vigilance, with an awareness that we do not harm others and we do not harm and hurt ourselves, we do not need to feel shame or guilt about ugly thoughts that we have—those ugly thoughts, feelings, emotions.

Because we have been exposed to particular things, whether we know it or not, that were very unpleasant, that does not mean that this is what we are. We are what we do with our intelligence and our feelings with an absence of harm or the intent to harm. We are not looking here for excuses and rationales for our conduct. We're attempting to understand what we have to work with. We're given all the necessary equipment for joy and happiness and contentment and everything is given to us to live a good, pleasant, satisfying life.

We need to see that despite the many thoughts and impulses that we regard as ugly and unpleasant, these thoughts do not diminish us; and as long as we see and control our actions and our deeds, and our feelings toward others so that we do not cause harm, we are not diminished.

Meaning

With your permission, will you consider that many of us wonder at times if life is meaningful or if it is just something that we go through by chance.

Everyone's life has purpose, meaning, significance. Whether this purpose is realized is our decision. What we decide to do with our lives consists of many decisions, sometimes many decisions within a given day. We are constantly making decisions in regard to the purpose and meaning of our individual lives.

Our significance does not require some kind of a fame, being a well-known person. This is not essential. This may happen. Okay, it happens but whether it does or not, does not signify that this particular person's life is meaningful. All lives are meaningful and worthy if we

want our lives to be meaningful. Our
achievements do not require great
talents, great efforts but they do require
thoughtfulness and being aware of
ourselves and others continuously,
vigilantly.

Some of us may regard life as a
cosmic joke or accident without purpose
and we may so decide. Everyone makes
their own decisions.The continuous
effort to maintain and be useful,
purposeful, enjoyable in our society
requires using our intelligence. It does
not require great intelligence. We do not
need to be a physicist or a brain
surgeon. Anyone—man, woman, and
child—is given enough intelligence to
lead a purposeful, satisfying life.
Intelligence and using our intelligence
requires some effort on our part, some
action on our part. It's much easier to be
indifferent, let life slide by, making the
minimum effort to live. We can do that.
But we are limiting ourselves and
exercising in effect a self-judgment. Joy,
happiness, satisfaction do require some
effort—not a great deal. You're not
building the pyramids singlehandedly.
You're not devising new rules to further
explain quantum mechanics. You're not

doing things that you are not capable or qualified to do in your efforts, your daily efforts to live with yourself, to have respect for yourself so that you may have respect for others.

This cannot be overemphasized. It is so easy to be indifferent, to be casual, to be non-thinking because there is some effort necessary in making decisions, considering others, considering yourself—how you proceed, how you talk with others, how you live with others, how you work with others. This requires a constant vigilance. This is not a painful or difficult thing to do but it does require our awareness, alertness; a consciousness that tells you you do not expect harm from others and you do not present or give harm to others. There is a phrase that my Dad used on many occasions to me and it is apt. It is meaningful. Keep on going.

A Vision of God

*A*gain into the breech with your permission.

I want to try to describe, try to tell each of you personally what I think is the life force which for the sake of brevity, simplicity I refer to as God. This vision is something I believe entirely, completely.

Although these thoughts and commentaries are for the most part philosophical, it seems when we're discussing life and what it means or may not mean to us, we always tend to become metaphysical. Or we end up talking with religious overtones even though we're trying to talk about it in a philosophical sense—in a way that is acceptable or can be allowed by all people. I am not proposing one particular vision or idea or interpretation or belief—I'm just mentioning or trying to bring together what I can see.

We all have our versions of God and the constant awareness of God's presence is something that I think and believe is going on all the time with all of us. There is none of us that He, She or It ignores or leaves alone despite the great pain or anguish or grief that may be occurring with many of us. Much of our difficulty is the random (and the careless) choices and decisions that mankind has made for centuries.

God intercedes at times I believe but we cannot expect a lot of instant intercession by Him to make things right. As individuals, we have been given freedom of choice. Now if we were interceded with, if we were interrupted every time we made a poor choice or incorrect decision, it would be similar to the child whose mother and father attempt to make many of the choices and decisions for the child. I believe this works out all right. I think it's correct as we raise children to do this. But at the same time we recognize the child needs to make his or her own choices and their own decisions.

We cannot expect a miracle every five minutes or every day of a particular kind that we think should occur. Because it doesn't occur in our life as quickly as we'd like or it doesn't occur at all in a way that we think it should, we get very unhappy with God. "Oh, He's not doing His job right. He's making a big mistake here."

The concept of error and God who is goodness do not coincide. You cannot have error and goodness or correctness simultaneously.

We have what we call arbitrarily error, apparent through mankind's choices and decisions. Mankind's choices and decisions may be seen as in error when we ignore our intelligence and that magic gift we've been given—conscience—which is an instant flash, an instant spark of intelligence that says it would be better to do it like this than like that. We all have this. We all know it. We all recognize it.

We cannot ignore that we are loved although we may. We cannot ignore that God too may be happy or unhappy. I believe He designed this life for happiness. There is some grief in life as things change particularly with people, as people change form, as they leave us momentarily, similar to the happiness or the unhappiness of saying good-bye. We feel a momentary sadness with our good-byes.

This does not mean that most of life is not to be enjoyed. Suffering and striving may occur but I do not believe this is God's idea. I think God's idea for us is peace, beauty, joy, and the pleasure of each other's company.

We need to recognize the phrase and what it means that we are all God's children. I don't think God has favorites. It would be very difficult, impossible I think, to pick out one child, one being who would have more meaning or who we would love more than another. Love is something that is not earned. I believe love is something that is allowed.

When we get close to God through our prayers, attitudes, joys, the nearness to God is not without its dangers.

Many people in the past and even today have been aware of the ecstasy of God's presence—the euphoria or exuberance of His or Her reality. The intoxication that is sensed and the contentment, all these feelings, because they are so strong and unusual, can be misunderstood or misused. These enormous, striking, brightly lit jolts of awareness of cosmic power that we may know do not give to any of us exclusive gifts.

God's closeness may be known to any and all of us at any time.

Faith, Belief, and Knowing

*T*his commentary is about faith, belief
and knowing and how we may arrive
at all three of these considerations. So
with your permission...
I will use the example of the infant
or young child at the age of about two, or
two and a half learning to walk to illus-
trate faith.
The parents are holding the child.
The child has been standing in its crib,
or attempting to stand in the buggy, and
of course does its best to wiggle out of
the high chair, or when you're holding it,
the child continues to stretch, push
away from you to try to land on its head,
or do some other kind of acrobatics. Now
the child at this moment trusts the parents. The parents are supporting the
child by its fingers so that its legs are
held up, supported by the fingers, the
hands of the parents. It's crawling a bit
on its two legs but is attempting to make

all kinds of movement: the legs sideways, back and forth, every way. But the child has enough faith to stand there, to be held and to attempt to move its feet in what will be its first steps. This I think constitutes faith.

Belief occurs when the child is held by one parent and has been walked about the house supported by one of the parent's hands or supported by a parent on each side as it attempts to toddle between them.

Then comes the great day when the parents sit apart from each other, one on one chair, one on another so that there's a distance of five feet or so and the child attempts to walk between them. It attempts to walk between the parents because—it may not be conscious of having a feeling of belief but whatever the child feels at the moment—I consider it belief, as it makes its effort to walk between its two parents. It may fall, get up, stumble the first few times but eventually the child does manage to walk or stumble on its two feet between its parents and as it continues, the child has more belief that it is capable of walking between the parents without stumbling and without falling. Then the child is, let's say, seven years old and the child now walks with its parents, runs about by itself, with his friends. He or she is free; moving about on two legs all by themselves, without thought, without a feeling of faith, without a feeling of belief, without wonderment, and without doubt. The child walks because the child knows he can walk. He doesn't consider it any longer to be a struggle.

This kind of knowing I consider to be necessary in regard to how we look at the world, the universe, how we look at each other, when we consider through our senses, through our means of knowing that creation is given and is a reality. We know the realities. We don't necessarily only have faith and belief which is vital in our life. We have a concept of *knowing*.

In this life and in our reflections and our considerations, knowing is what allows us to trust, to trust one another.

If we are asked about a particular individual, a friend, or a relative and we are asked the question, "Well how do you know you can trust that person?" It's an exceedingly difficult question to answer because we are back to the premise, back to the example of walking again. We don't think about walking or have faith or belief in walking, we know we can walk. When we are asked about our loved ones we do not have to consider some kind of proof of performance or credentials or consider what a lot of other people may think. We, in our own separate, private individuality, we know we can trust this particular loved one.

If we can carry the idea a bit further, it follows that if we can know, if we can love one, understand, appreciate, enjoy *one*, why should we consider that there's a limit—that there's only one?

All people have the sense of magnificence. They may not sense their own but we all have it and we all may know each other's constant magnificence.

Work

We work so that we may eat so that we may be.

Work is one of the most significant things that we do in our lifetime regardless of what form that work may take. Any work that is done has validity and meaning whether you are doing the work of a garbage collector or whether you are sitting behind a desk and working as president of a large, successful corporation.

Any work that we do may bring with it satisfactions which are very necessary for us during our life on this earth—satisfactions, because we know we're doing a particular task as well as we can, and with as much efficiency and intelligence and effort that we have. As we continue to do our work we may learn more about it. We may be able to perform our task in a more efficient way, a more satisfying way so that when we are through with our daily work and we are at home, we may be tangibly satisfied.

Work has been regarded at many times and in many instances as a dull drudgery and that the only reason we do it is so we may earn the means to obtain food and shelter. We need to look at work differently...no matter how dull or no matter how misplaced we may be in a particular type of work, knowing that we have capabilities that are sometimes much greater than the particular task that we are engaged in requires.

We need to see the value of working. We do oftentimes have circumstances when we are doing work that really isn't our field. We can work in other areas and at times we are doing work that we're not trained for, but it doesn't make any difference as far as the value, the quality, and the significance of the work itself is concerned. We may always change our jobs or get a better job, or what we call better. Better might consist of more pay, better expense accounts, longer vacations, or whatever particular things we desire. But work in itself has a value that does not require our approval of the particular task. All work that we may do—digging coal, planting corn, working in an assembly plant, baking bread—all work that we're doing or may do is essential to our particular way of life.

The work itself has its own value. So when I say that your work is just as worthy whether you may be hauling garbage or running a company, the feeling and attitude about the work does not mean that we in some way must judge and declare one job, one work superior to another.

All of us workers are of equal value. Someone has to sweep the streets. Someone has to answer the telephone. Someone has to sign the paychecks. We've got all these jobs that we may even prefer over the particular job that we have and that's fine, that's okay. If you find another job that you would rather do, that's fine. Do it but don't be ashamed of what you are doing. Don't be ashamed of your work as long as you realize that your work is not harming mankind but that your work is significant in a sense that it is a necessary task.

The president of the great

corporation goes home and even the person with that apparently significant job, even he may need to do some task around the house when servants are not available, or the machinery that's being used is broken down and he may even go so far as to cut the grass without feeling degradation.

We have at many times the wrong attitude toward work. People ask us what we do and we feel there is some sort of shame attached to it because we're not driving around in a nice, fine car, wearing elegant clothes and spending a lot of money and giving orders to many people. We relate this to ourselves as though our work reflects ourselves. No. The work can give you satisfactions even when it's a menial task. Menial. There is satisfaction in the fact that you are doing it and you are doing it well. We may wish to consider: Are we earning or making a living in the correct way?

The ancient ways that seemed to be exclusively hunting and fishing wouldn't fit today's industrialized nations. What is a correct way to provide food and shelter for ourselves and our families? Perhaps we need to look in other directions. There isn't any job that requires that you be ashamed of doing it. This is almost another way of saying that one person is better than another. One job is preferable to another—yes—but the work itself, regardless of whether it is *preferable* is of value in itself and it doesn't take away from your meaning and your significance and your value because you at the moment happen to be sweeping the streets.

Admitting Our Humanity

*Y*et again, with your permission.
If I were separate from or did not
regard myself as part of humanity I
would not believe that my life on this
earth had any meaning or significance.
In other words, if we do not recognize
our connection with others, any others,
all others, we are limiting ourselves. We
are not admitting our humanness and in
not admitting our own we do not admit
the humanity, the significance, and the
meaning of others.

We go through life oftentimes at a
very hectic pace, sometimes humdrum.
For most of us as we experience ten
years and we look back upon it, it
appears to be one year. Thirty years is
five. And so our relationship and our
thinking about time is very misleading.
To maintain our awareness of others and
of ourselves often we need to consider

our basic needs and requirements relating first of all to ourselves and then others. I in no way am implying selfishness here. I am stating rather the reality that you really can't do much with or enjoy others unless self-recognition is occurring first, in your uniqueness, your own difference. And then because you are a *one and only* there's a strong awareness of a feeling of separation from others.The separation from others is true, is valid but it doesn't deprive us in any way of enjoying and sharing and knowing others.

We need not be fearful of this concept of loneliness. All of our feelings and our consideration of values, morality, ethics, all of these which the human mind encompasses and uses and considers are not our inventions.

We may arrange these things in different ways. We may insist on a priority set-up—one thing comes before another— but really what we are doing and what we are to each other is our first consideration.

We know and we may respect ourselves which is a priority to respecting others. It is out of balance really not to acknowledge yourself and your value, and at the same time try to work out some sort of a compatible relationship with another or others that you respect and admire. You feel that they can substitute in some way for what you do not feel about yourself. These things happen. This is temporary. Children do it as they are growing. The dependency relationship can be natural but it can also be extreme and unnatural when it continues when we are no longer children.

All of these things that we have which I suggested earlier: emotions, values, our intelligence, all of this is given. It really doesn't make any difference how it's given or how we think it was given. It was given. It is a knowing. It's what is.

We may regard life as being brought about originally by God, our Creator, or we may believe in the big bang solution that life is an accident of chemistry and physics; or we may regard it as a process of movement through many species of things until we manage to attain the standard that we now call human. It doesn't make any difference what you regard as the cause or the beginning or the influence or whatever it is that gives you a concept of goodness. You can call it the Force, the Great Source, or the Creator, whatever term you might use. We're all aware that we have all of these emotions and we are aware that we have the concept of goodness. We all have the concept of unhappiness, happiness, joy, grief, fear. Fear is a very necessary emotion.

Now we're going to do some things that appear to be off and we do them with the best of motives and we need to remember de Sales' law, the road to hell is paved with good intentions.

We do all sorts of things with the idea that this act is good. This is for the general good of humanity or this act is good for us therefore it's good, period. We need always to be aware—before we make any moves in life with ourself or others—that the idea of balance and stability means that we look it over first before we act. It's not just impulse, impulsive actions, with no reflection. Of course there are times of emergency and survival when you are forced to, required by the pressures that exist to act quickly, and you don't have time to think it over, then you have to make a move immediately. This situation exists. It happens. Fortunately or unfortunately, it does occur.

Everything we may do is important whether or not it is based on reflection or necessary impulse. Although this may appear to be a contradiction, much of life's movement requires contradiction.

Wondering

With your permission.
All our great religions believe in God, in goodness.

Why do all the religions not get together and state repeatedly what they have in common—that they are of one mind in regard to God and goodness? Why do religions, supposedly believing the same thing, appear to compete with each other?

Integrity

With your gracious permission. I want to comment on what the word integrity means. Your integrity. Your personal, individual, unique integrity. Your gathered-together self.

We all have been given abilities, talents, sense of awareness, and with these gifts we need to understand and appreciate more and see the significance of mankind, of each of us; not that this is pinning medals on yourself or pinning medals on other people arbitrarily or applauding when there is no reason for applause. Integrity is something that we all have and we maintain integrity throughout our lives and continue to see how significant and how splendid each person is through their integrity. So we need to understand our sense of integrity, what it means, how it may be applied and particularly how it may be seen and understood.

We have been given at birth many things from our ancestors, our parents, our relatives, our friends, neighbors, teachers, those people who are interested in us. All of those things that we have been given at birth; our senses, our instinctive appreciation of beauty and harmony; our awareness at birth of when we're comfortable and uncomfortable and what makes us feel this way. Things that please us are comfortable. Things that displease us are uncomfortable.

Throughout life we could not recognize our significance and the significance of others if we had not had the privileges and benefits of education in any form. All those bits of knowing. All those wonderful things of civilizing institutions that allow us to become our entire whole selves. Our whole selves. The undivided self, the wholeness of each of us and our appreciation of this wholeness that we have and everyone else has is what we call integrity.

According to the dictionary, the word means the quality or state of being complete. Now with all of these things that I have mentioned, we see a completeness. We may have felt very incomplete, scattered, dissatisfied, wondering, "What's missing, what's missing, what's wrong? Why do I feel frustrated? Why do I feel constantly puzzled? Why do I feel incomplete? Why do I feel like I'm left out, I'm lonely?"

All these things can be understood quickly and immediately when you recognize that each person has been given the gift of integrity. And if he or she gathers this bountiful harvest of the magnificence of all these qualities that have greater value than anything else on earth, gathers all these qualities together in their moral state—then we may see each other and as we see each other, we see ourselves. What a viewing, a comfortable viewing this is! We recognize each other and we recognize each other's integrity and sense of integrity.

The word is not baffling. We do not need an intense struggle, or training of mental agility. We may put all these scattered pieces together and see them as you see an entity that is yourself. In a broader way than just your experience, you may be able to experience the thoughts, the joys, the significance, even the experiences of others. All we need is the ability to read. In the past, over the centuries, we needed the ability to hear and remember. This is limited. It does not give us the strength and the capacity that we have with our vast spirit. Our attitude, our spiritual attitude can be viewed in a broader way through our ability and our continuous examination of much of life through reading.

This doesn't mean that we go through life without experiences. We don't curl up in a corner and read from this day on. We do not say that there are only particular things to be read. We read in a spiritual sense that which is enjoyable, beautiful, magnificent.

It may not be the greatest book ever written. It may be something very common, very ordinary. But within it we do see the spark, the divine spark that tells us this is written and this is expressed by a person like myself, another who is equal to me or has the beauty, or gives me the enjoyment as I look or as I read, that allows me to see others. And by reflection may I enjoy the pleasure of seeing myself.

Violence

Without apology, again I need your permission.

We all have, all of us, have the answers, the means to solve all our problems, the vast problems that mankind has been subject to throughout the ages. And we've had the answers to our problems for many ages. But oftentimes we act like we as one solitary individual cannot do much about these great difficulties that mankind seems to endure rather than solve.

We are all born with all of our capabilities to treat each other in a way that does not harm or hurt each other. The capabilities to do things well—in a pleasing, satisfying, peaceful way. We also have the capabilities to hurt each other, to insult, to criticize, to break each other's bones, to kill each other. And because we have the capabilities to inflict harm, is that what these capabilities are for?

We know each of us would not like to have our nose broken or be pushed around or killed, injured in any way by others. We all know that. We can all appreciate that and yet down through the ages including today because we have capabilties to do harm we say then it must be okay in some way. It must be all right if we're capable of doing it. If there were anything about it that weren't okay we wouldn't have these capabilities—which is ridiculous. And yet this is how we act.

If we're capable of something that means it's okay to do it. If you need something and someone else has it, take it. We have all kinds of excuses and reasons. We can rationalize any act of terror and say it's all right under the circumstances, it's okay. Napolean was reputed to have said, You cannot make an omelette without breaking a few eggs. The only problem is you would not like to be one of the eggs that is broken.

We have said that mankind has ideas and a system that says one family is better or superior to another, one group of families is better or superior to another.

These are ideas. Who said so? Who made it okay? Because one family is stronger, has more money, more guns, more power it means, of course, they're supposed to be the number ones? There are no number ones. This is a myth and an illusion that has hindered and stopped mankind from achieving any kind of civilization that is ongoing, significant, and meaningful.

Each civilization, throughout the thousands of years that civilized efforts have been made, has fallen. None of them lasted. I think the reason they didn't last is quite apparent. We need to recognize in our daily life that everything we do is important. Cleaning our fingernails, tying our shoes, talking to our children, going to work, making decisions. There isn't anything that each of us does through our daily lives that is not important.

We say through particular achievements one person is more than another, more important, more meaningful. This is another illusion that we know is incorrect. We know in our hearts and minds that we are not more than any other. The only thing that has any significance is to recognize the value and significance of each other regardless of the power, authority, the medals, the awards that any particular person may have. We know the emptiness of an accomplishment if it does not give us the satisfaction of knowing we have lived with joy and peace and understanding with our fellow man.

The Individual Spirit

*Y*our permission allows me to continue.

The growth of the spirit, the climate of the spirit occurs while we're here on earth. And I am aware of the difficulties that we have with our spirit. Many of our spirits stay narrow, confined. They do not develop and grow as full, to their completeness. We may catch glimpses as we're growing up. We see children and momentarily we get a glimpse of the spirit there—their obvious joy and satisfaction. But much of the climate of the spirit, the necessary parts of the climate for the growth and development of the spirit is a feeling of well-being, satisfaction: the feeling that you have when you're not thinking about the grief that's going on or the poor decisions, the confusion, the incorrect choices, the bills that we have to pay tomorrow, our wonderment about how we are going to handle some difficulty. When we have these things out of our minds for the moment we have this feeling, and we've all experienced it, we all know what it is, this feeling that we call well-being. At that moment we have this sense of joy which is so vital to nourish the growth and development of what we are. Our spiritual self.

We have seen in the past that there are some spirits that we wonder about. The spirit seems so unhappy. The spirit appears to us to be misshapen, poorly formed, miserable and we need to wonder about it. I think this stems from a denial, whether it be deliberate, unconscious, or accidental but a denial of goodness. Our need for goodness is greater than our need for fresh air, for water. It's more than that because without a concept and a realization of the significance of goodness our life here on earth doesn't have much significance. When I say goodness I mean the sense of virtues, morality, ethics, fair play, the culmination of what we call God. When we do not have, or when we do not believe that there is a need for goodness, and we deny it by saying, "Well

that won't work. That's not realistic, pragmatic." Whatever the so-called reasons,
this puts a definite blight on the spirit.

We see people who have allowed
their spirits to develop and grow who do
believe that goodness has meaning even
though we cannot weigh and measure it,
and we have a tough time proving it.
We've seen people, we've known people
who are a pleasure to be around. They're a
joy to be with, not because they tell funny
stories and they are amusing but because
of their stability, their happiness, their joy,
their satisfactions, their inner strengths.
We see it developing—spirit.

What I am attempting to speak of as
a spirit is what I think we may all attain
in its fullness, that the sense of well-being
that we're aware of—that only happens
momentarily it seems on this earth—will
become more constant in our life, more
solid, more substantial as we allow ourselves to see and recognize that all of us
have spiritual value, spiritual *being:* and
it isn't something to be taken lightly. Some
may say, "Well I can't stick a label on it. I
can't really grasp it so it isn't real." It is
the essence. It is what you are.

To accept your spirit and your sense
of well-being and the meaning and the

significance of others is the joy that allows us to know that fair play is not a myth. Fair play can occur and will occur on this earth as more people accept that along with our other needs is the basic need to know goodness.

Values

With your permission.
I believe the first value we should consider is the value of self. The value of ourselves. We have been given a body, a mind, a spirit. To consider value as a human being we need to look first at the children. We may see their beauty, their magnificence, their wonderment. We can see and recognize value in being. As we grow older it's more difficult to see value in ourselves and others because of the actions, interactions between people. Usually we conceal much of our magnificence, our meaning, and our significance because of the confusion and the chaos that exists in the world and our intelligence, our mental ability is ignored.

We are not aware with constant vigilance, intelligent vigilance of our meaning and the meaning of others. If we do not utilize our intelligence constantly then in all of the actions we have with other people we're going to have difficulties.

Our brain wasn't given to us by chance or accident. We have the most highly developed brain in all the world. As far as life is concerned on other planets we do not know about any intelligence there yet to any degree—we have theories. We have been given this brain with which to choose and make decisions. Whenever we lose sight of the value of a single human being or of ourselves, our intelligence may as well be in neutral... not functioning. Not working. We cannot do or live or enjoy whenever we fail to acknowledge others or we ignore the value of ourselves as part of a judgment sequence.

There isn't anything on this earth that is more valuable than a human being.

I think this is what many teachers through the ages were trying to get across to many people, to many cultures throughout the ages. Although it appears obvious as I think it is, it is often overlooked. Many of us say, "I cannot afford morality. I cannot afford to look at the other fellow as I look at myself. I have to eat first." Yeah. Yeah, you have to eat;

whether it's first or second doesn't make any difference but you do have to, in the process, eat in peace, living together without famine, living together with enjoyment, living together with the recognition of each of our values without considering a measurement of values such as achievements or abilities.

All mankind has value regardless of his or her achievements. We have the basic value without having to prove our value. We have value because we have been given life. We've been given a mind. We've been given a body and we haven't been given these things randomly or haphazardly or incidentally.

I believe all values and all ideals are attainable by mankind. I think mankind has the ability to live in an ideal world. I think we can strive and decide and achieve a world that's significant and enjoyable as we live with a continuing and vigilant intellectual effort. All of us have intellectual capacities.

We can achieve and we can live as long as we understand and maintain and consider the value of each other. This isn't some mysterious, complex problem here. But what we have done through ignoring our meaning and each other's meaning—we've managed to attain quite an interesting arrangement in this world that isn't particularly joyous all the time. In fact, much of the time it is not very satisfying. It is not as meaningful as it can be. You are meaningful. Everyone is meaningful. It should not be ignored. Or forgotten. Or overlooked. It should be like freedom. The constant vigilance, the constant consideration.

Freedom of Choice

What mankind is doing to the earth is ugly as we can see today. We can see now many of our beautiful streams and rivers are open sewers but they're open sewers because the factories, the industry that pollutes them appears to be necessary so that we may support ourselves and our families. We need to eat so that we may be.

We see the polluted air from much of our machinery and we say, "Well this is necessary so that we can get to work so that we keep warm so that we can survive with power and energy."

So on one hand, all of the choices that we have are economic choices for survival. At the same time, it appears to be unhealthy, dangerous perhaps, because of what happens with all of these collective industries: poisonous smoke, byproducts that pollute our streams, lakes, oceans. Are our choices proper or improper?

So we need to consider, always, *always*—we cannot retire our awareness. Our senses are given to us to understand, to communicate, to realize that we need to know what we are doing and what others are doing always so that we do not do things that are dangerous to ourselves and others, so that we continue to be alert, aware of others.

Courtesy for example is awareness of others; not to the point of being obsequious but so that we are constantly saying that we do recognize each other. We consider that perhaps God, Allah, the Great Spirit has been unduly criticized for many of the acts and many of the problems and much of our worldly unhappiness. We blame and criticize God for doing these things. We say, "Well, we should have freedom of choice," but at the same time, "He should intercede."

Well, make up your mind.

Knowledge
and Intelligence

*A*gain and yet again with your permission.

Knowledge and intelligence are not the same. Many people have acquired, studied, learned, and have a great deal of knowledge. Knowledge in itself has very little meaning unless it is utilized beneficially through our intelligence.

Let us look at this division between intelligence and knowledge. They are not one and the same. We may know many things and know not what to do with the information. We may have a little information and the little we do have we may apply very well to our lives.

Knowledge today is easy to acquire. We have books, libraries, encyclopedias, and quick access on the internet. We can find out about any subject—many books on practically everything. Many of us regard knowledge as dangerous. Knowledge is only dangerous if it's misused, if it's used to harm, to hurt, to manipulate, take advantage of another in painful or injurious ways. This is a misuse of knowledge. In other words, it means knowledge is not being applied intelligently.

Many of us regard any kind of intellectual endeavor as dull or even meaningless. Whatever we have learned, whatever we have acquired with all our senses may be used throughout our lives, even though we cannot foresee or anticipate how much of our general knowledge may be used. Whenever we put forth effort to acquire knowledge (and knowledge has been known as power), we need to consider constantly in what way are we using our knowledge.

If our knowledge only benefits ourselves—is that enough? Is that okay? Yes. It may be but when we consider ourselves we need to consider others too. Have I got so much that I

have more food than I can ever eat?
Have I got more clothing than I can
ever wear? Have I got more houses than
I can really use? These things need to
be considered as we go through life and
we strive to achieve some material
gains and take care of ourselves, our
loved ones, maybe another generation.

So intelligence is vital, necessary
to be used with our knowledge to strive
for a balance, a sense of proportion in
life. Do I need the biggest slice of the
pie? It is necessary that all of us have a
slice of the pie. We need to see and
apply our knowledge intelligently so
that we may all live in a beneficial and
satisfying way.

With our intelligence and
knowledge we can recognize and
appreciate the value and significance of
others. If our knowledge and
intelligence blind us from the
appreciation of others, we are not using
our intelligence and knowledge
properly. All of us are connected to each
other. The way we are together is often
obvious. We know it with family
immediately. But most of our
connections with each other are all
unknown. But so we may all enjoy and

appreciate our lives we all need to use our intelligence for our mutual greater good.

Fear

*A*llow me.
We may be doing what we can each day—respecting ourselves and others—and in the midst of our daily lives a loved one dies in an accident, through illness, old age, whatever. At this moment we will perhaps feel that life is a pretty dismal arrangement. Life is not worthwhile. It doesn't come out right. It's not being done properly. It's agony. And these feelings of emptiness, pain, frustration we may all have through life. The grief may last for a long time. We may consider, "What's the use? What's the use of trying to live in a way that's thoughtful, meaningful toward myself and others? Life seems to be at this moment a study in futility. It's nowhere," and in our pain these feelings can be recognized and understood by all of us.

When an infant is born, I believe it has a rather frightening time. Everything in its life is radically changed from what it was when its mother was carrying the child. The child is frightened as we are frightened and disturbed when it appears we have lost a loved one forever. The infant, as it continues to grow—become a year old, two years old, three years old—the infant is frightened of many things: sudden movements, loud noises, radical changes as we are when we are in the midst of grief. And yet we protect the infant so it doesn't put its hands on the hot stove, it does not try to swallow things that are indigestible and the many things that an infant considers to do that we know are painful and injurious to the child.

We can understand it. We can understand the fears of an infant. We can understand fear when we are sitting down to the dinner table and a tiger jumps through the window and lands in our midst. And we have enough fear so that we realize that it might be a good idea to get out of the way.

Now as we go through life some frightening things happen to us and we're very concerned about living with an awareness of ourselves and our actions and our connection with others and the need to get along with others. We wonder if our daily efforts are worthwhile in the midst of grief.

As we continue in spite of our difficulties and our wonderment about the correctness of living, we need to consider: it worked out all right for the infant. There are many things we do not understand (not that I believe there are great mysteries that we will not or that we are not capable of understanding) but as long as we persevere with our feelings, with our intelligent feelings toward others, our respectful feelings toward ourselves and others, we can see that we need not be disturbed about what appears to be a poorly arranged life.

Accidents or frightening illnesses, whatever, we will be all right. We will live, we will enjoy and we will continue in the only way that's meaningful, in the only way that makes life worthwhile: in our consideration of self and others. In our daily struggle for food and shelter it may occur that we will realize and we will know that although we may at one

time no longer have our present need
and our striving for food and shelter, we
will always need and we will always
have the company of our loved ones.

Failure

With your hopeful permission...
We all have our ideas about what
a successful life is and what failure is.
Each of us is the only one who can say
things to ourselves about failure. No one
else has that right.

If you are comparing yourself to
others or looking at the guy or gal next
door, someone you hear about in the
newspapers, magazines, TV, some great
success and you haven't achieved your
particular goals, this does not mean that
you have failed.

In life, it doesn't matter how
many awards you may be given, no
matter how much applause, pats on the
back. No matter how many cheers and
hurrahs for you go on—this may never
occur in your life. That's okay.

A life that is successful means
putting forth effort, using your
intelligence, your awareness, trying to

learn more—collect more knowledge that you consider necessary in your life and in your endeavors. Now your endeavors, your work, your strivings don't seem, in your eyes and in others', but particularly yours—just don't seem to measure up or be enough, not satisfying, feel frustrated, not enough feeling of accomplishment. Keep in mind, at all times, that while you are putting forth the daily effort of living, as long as you know and you are aware that you haven't brought harm or injury to others—you're doing okay.

This is not an easy thing to do. We haven't much practice down through the years, through generations, but as long as that's what you are striving to do— no matter how many times you don't make the moves with others as well as you would like to make them—as long as you are trying, putting forth the effort to recognize the significance of others. As long as you maintain and allow and recognize your value, your own meaning; and your value and meaning that does not require money, power, position. If these things occur, if you achieve these things and you're aware of others, not stepping on someone, not harming them, fine, great. Even if you do not achieve what we commonly call success, keep on going, don't stop.

Continue with your efforts in your way, in your own individual way to live a life in which you know—this is the only thing that's significant is that *you* know—you have done whatever you could all through the years to respect yourself and respect the meaning of others. This may not sound like much alongside a million dollars or a great title or some gold medals. It may not sound like much. But it is the only thing of value no matter how many millions you may have or how many medals. Your value does not come to you through the applause, the credits, the awards, the opinions of others.

Your opinion of yourself and what you do is all that has meaning. You're the one who calls the shots. You're the one in your life who can say, "I'm a failure." This premise does not belong to someone else. This concept, this idea, this label, this expression doesn't belong to you either. This is a judgment. A self-judgment. You are not entitled to it. You do as you can and do as well as you can with your abilities and intelligence, your awareness. You consider your meaning and the meaning of all others—the ones you know, come in contact with, hear about. You, in this universe, are what's significant. As long as you are doing everything you can with your ability and your intelligence to appreciate and care for (and by *care for*, I do not mean supporting in a material sense—you may do that too) I mean when I say *care for* that you're aware of every other human being.

Failure is a very misused word and it is not a brand and it is not a label that can be seen and it has nothing to with our culture or ethnic background, skin color, nothing at all to do with it. When we seek to attach this kind of label, significance, this word to ourselves and to others, what are we doing here? We're saying "Stop! I've had too much. I've put out too much effort. I never had a break, I never had an opportunity. I've had too many injuries. I've had stress. I've been abused..." and on and on.

Yes, that may be true. That may happen to many of us. But what is of value and what is of significance is *keep on going*.

Animals

 gain with your thoughtful
permission.

Our ancestors long ago did not live
in urban areas we call towns or villages.
For the most part they were in scattered
bands, family units and they observed
and learned from animals, birds, insects,
all the things around them.

One thing they did begin to note
and that they respected and in fact
oftentimes worshipped were animals
because animals seemed to know what
they were doing the majority of the time.
They knew how to survive, how to
protect the young, how to protect herds
if they were that type of animal.
Animals seemed to know.

Mankind, with his greater
intelligence, often didn't seem to know.
He was confused often as we still are
today in many areas so he was conscious

of animals and the animal social structure and the animals' physical dominance of a territory and the animals' leadership and their fierceness and their anger and their philosophy and their courage. He noticed all these things in animals and yet many times mankind was in doubt about his own knowing.

Animals do not have the intelligence of humans. They are predetermined through what we call instincts, through their more sensitive senses, the information gathering senses. They know what to do, not in a thoughtful, reflective way but instinctively, almost immediately as though they're programmed—as though it's all set up, it's all done, this know-how to act within their particular life structure. Yet they oftentimes do things that seem thoughtful or spontaneous... not predetermined.

Now as I say, this was very impressive to man to see this knowing. Early mankind developed a language, as crude as it may have been, but he hadn't yet developed a way of storing up, accumulating, keeping knowledge—things that he had learned, that he could tell others; and mankind did for a long time use memory. Instead of a written language, many ancients had prodigious, great memories. They could tell the young what they had learned, what they had observed and pass it on from generation to generation.

Until mankind developed a written language—words that were portable, that could be stored—he more than likely scratched some marks in the mud as his particular sign or he may have carved symbols: animals, pictures in the beginning, a form of writing. To record numbers, he may have put nicks in a piece of wood, tied knots in a vine.

Anyway, we developed words, written words—a language, so that we could accumulate knowledge, information and we could see that with an accumulation of knowledge we didn't have to go through each procedure, learn each thing all over again. We learned more intricate things, more intelligent things other than keep your hand out of the campfire because it is hot and the wood is burning.

We learned and saw that much of what the animals did utilized a very small amount of intelligence. It didn't require a lot of intelligence but it did require a lot of emotional response. Animals demonstrated anger. They demonstrated affection. They demonstrated a form of bluffing, blustering, demonstrated contentment but most of what they were capable of we would regard as emotional responses.

So animals have knowing and we for centuries respected the knowing. Particularly impressive was the absence of doubt. They seemed to respond well in so many areas of their lives and they didn't doubt what they were doing. They weren't confused, so as mankind observed and developed his intelligence, he learned to accept other people. I think in the beginning just for the means of survival. Our ancestors saw that doing things together developed a more substantial, secure way to live. But they also began to recognize each other as having value; not necessarily merely enemies or ones who would take their food or drive them away from wherever they were trying to live but they began to see their fellow man as having a significance and meaning in a possible cooperative way, as with hunting and fishing for example.

Now we attempt to learn and get along with each other and enjoy each other but oftentimes it seems difficult, tedious, impossible. There is an old Chinese, I believe, proverb that says, "The longest, most difficult journey begins with a single step." And when we are looking for ways to live with each other, to respect each other, we need to understand and appreciate that our efforts, no matter how small, minute, unknown except to ourselves and those we meet, that those small, seemingly small efforts are the way that we can live together with enjoyment, satisfactions and completeness.

Although mankind imitated and worshipped animals for centuries, it is not necessary for us today to imitate the fierceness and the cruelty that is necessary so that the animals may survive.

Who and What We Are

With your permission, let's examine what is meaningful.

In the beginning, the first part is how or what we see as ourselves. It is very difficult to care for others, to appreciate others, to see others when we do not see ourselves as meaningful and significant and it does not depend—our significance, our meaning—on achievements, symbols of accomplishment, on applause. We all do what we can do and it's not necessary that we all try to be the same in the area of accomplishments. We all do not have to be professional people. We do not have to achieve particular goals and aims that are regarded by most of us, the public, as being significant.

Achievements fine. Becoming, or being a person who is considered a significant, meaningful member of society is wonderful but do not lose sight of yourself in this. Others' applause, others' judgment or condemnation does not mean that's what we are. You are not dependent upon others for the individuality, the entity, the *you*, the *me* that you are. If we allow ourselves to be persuaded to do this or do that, the persuasion may be with all goodness or great, fine intentions; the ultimate reason for doing and for being is the meaning that we have for ourselves.

As I attempted to say a long time ago, in caring, appreciating, understanding others, the difficulty is how we feel about ourselves. Not all the time, not a hundred percent. That's not necessary as long as you feel occasionally that you have meaning.

The general framework that we live in, that we call civilized life, permits us movement, does not impair our individuality unless we allow it to. We can believe, we can become the kind of person who we do not need to feel conceit or egotistical about but a person who we can enjoy, a person who we can like. Each of us has that capability. Each of us was born with the emotions, the intelligence to be likable, useful regardless of what worldly status or category people might put us in.

As I have said, any job, any work that you have that does not harm others, that does not interfere with others and their well-being is significant...whether it's washing dishes, scrubbing floors, working with things as long as what you are doing, your performance, your work is done in a way that you know you are doing a good job, what you regard as a good job. It is meaningful to you to do the good job even though the job is not regarded as significant in the framework of our civilized life. It is an area that has been defined in many ways—what I mean by a civilized life, it means recognizing the need for order, minimizing the chaos and confusion, and realizing that we can read so that we can expand our awareness of others. Reading expands what we can do. It allows us to see more about ourselves and we can work and be and enjoy without feeling we are lost, adrift.

Our value does not depend upon the interest of others. The indifference of others is not anything that can deter us from being—as long as we can continue to know and to do, and to share some ideas, some feelings, some thinking with others. We know that we are attached. We know that we are a part of a framework we call civilization. We know that we are among our fellow men and women.

No One is More Than Me

With your permission, allow me to say, no one is more than me. No one is less than me. No one is the same as me. This concept, these words are necessary so that each of us may understand our particular meaning and significance.

Mankind has endeavored for many centuries to attempt to live the good life. We have difficulty in getting along with each other, understanding our individual uniqueness, our cultural uniqueness. We have had difficulty. I think that in order for us to understand each other we need to realize the value and significance of self-respect.

It is very difficult to love another, to care for another, to understand another, to get along with another, if we regard ourselves as unworthy or even meaningless. So that we may be able to get along in this life, it is necessary to see that a particular talent, great intellect, remarkable memory, or ability to do things (that it seems other people cannot do as well) are talents that some of us are given and that's fine. That's okay. But that does not denote superiority over anyone else: the person who does not apparently have any particular outstanding talents, who does not have a great intellect, does not have a prodigious recall, vast stores of knowledge, or does not have a strong physical advantage. Because this person does not appear to have these talents, it does not lessen their value.

We need to use our intelligence, all of us. The brain does not stop functioning. It does not take a rest or vacation. We need to use it and apply it constantly when we have anything at all to do with another individual or group of individuals. We need to see our significance and recognize theirs.

It does not make any difference if the other person or persons are of a particular ethnic group—darker skin, lighter skin. Our skin color, our attitudes, our beliefs, our considerations, our cultural habits cannot give us superiority over others.

Our greatest difficulty down through the ages has been to understand and accept people who speak different languages, have different habits from our own. There is no one culture that is superior to another, one color superior to another nor are there any cultures that are less than another. Until we allow ourselves to see that our value is not based upon ideas of superiority or inferiority we will not be able to recognize another person. We will even have difficulty recognizing ourselves.

This life was meant to be enjoyed. It is very difficult to enjoy life in the midst of man-made trials and tribulations, economic disasters, wars, contention, and strife with each other.

We are all born as separate, unique individuals. Each of us different, as different as each snowflake, each grain of sand, microscopically different—the sand and the snowflake but in the vastness of the human mind, and the human soul, we are different from each other. That difference, that uniqueness allows us to make decisions and to consider, to attempt to examine, to understand ourselves and others. Without this we cannot love and without love life has no meaning. It is empty no matter our so-called great power, wealth, or significance. Unfortunately, what we all share and what causes us much consistent difficulty is ignorance. Many of us can have considerable intelligence and yet possess a great amount of ignorance. In light, in knowing, all people are possible.

Solving Problems

With your permission, allow problems to be fully and completely stated so we know what to solve.

We are told every day by newspapers, television, radio, magazines, books, that we have great problems. You know them all by heart I'm sure—the ozone hole in the sky, overpopulation, the environment. We are told also that these problems are just about impossible to solve, just too big for us. These problems that we have are brought about through fear, greed, thoughtless actions. But each of us has the ability and we can solve all these so-called impossible problems.

We have problems. Whenever we ignore or are indifferent to ourselves or to others or whenever we do not consider that our feelings, our thoughts, our actions are meaningful—all our thoughts and actions, what we do with each other, how we feel about ourselves—then we have problems.

We can and we will, if we want to, solve all these problems. Each of us in our own individual way will be a part of the solution to these problems. We will persist and consider ourselves and others in a way where we do not cause harm or injury to others. That's what we start with. That's basic. If we are indifferent to ourselves and others we're not going to solve much of anything.

We were not granted, we were not given the privilege, the luxury, the thoughtlessness of being anything we please no matter its effect on ourselves and others—as if we could do it with some kind of immunity—that's okay, it won't make any difference. It's just a little thing. Very little things, we cannot ignore forever.

When we look at life and we look at the beauty around us and we look at the enjoyment we can have with each other and we look at the charm and the fascination of a child—how can we consider in any kind of a reasonable way that all this magnificence is just here for nothing?

We know the difference. We know the difference between something that is beautiful and something that is ugly. We know when we commit a particular act and this act is satisfying and enjoyable to ourselves and others, this is a thing of beauty.

And when we do something that's thoughtless and inconsiderate, we know ugliness can occur. None of these things is beyond our comprehension or our ability to understand. We know what's going on.

If we inhibit our intelligence, if we distract it through the various means that mankind has played with down through the ages; if we dull our intelligence and our feelings through stimulants, through alcohol, drugs, doing things in an extreme way; doing anything that mars or distracts or inhibits or blurs our intelligence, we're not doing ourselves or others a favor.

If we are injured, if we are ill, in an accident, something like this, then it is of neccessity. We need an operation, we're going to be zonked out for a while. We're going to be sedated, we're going to

be unconscious, we're going to be in a
state where the pain, the trauma of
whatever is being operated on,
whatever the injury is being put on hold
for the moment. But through our daily
lives, our daily lives, our actions that
blur our intelligence are very
dangerous. Dangerous to ourselves and
others.

We can solve and we can handle
all of our problems. All of mankind's
problems. We have the intelligence, we
have the ability, we have the heart. We
have the mind and we are capable of
great love and we will solve our
problems and we will keep on going.

We need to always consider that
when we bring all our problem-solving
abilities, we also bring our prejudice,
our blindness, and preconceived correct
and incorrect ideas. So we need
enlightenment, prayer, and to keep on
going.

Emotions

With your permission...
We all have our individual
emotions and intelligence. We all feel
joy, satisfaction, anger, frustration.
When we consider the two ideas—
emotions and intelligence—much of the
time we utilize our emotions first of all
rather than combining them with our
intelligence. We do things through our
emotions. I think the emotions are the
starting point of most of our actions and
later our thoughts. Emotions and
intelligence overlap.

Our intelligence allows us much of
the time to hopefully control, to act as a
stabilizer for us to maintain a sense of
balance, proportion. When we look at
things, make decisions, consider
ourselves and others, we may have
many emotional feelings that are

incorrect as well as correct. By incorrect I mean the emotions of harming, injuring, hurting another.

When we look at what we do with each other throughout life it is our intelligence—and all of us have intelligence—our intelligence which allows us to make decisions that are correct in spite of our emotions which are pushing us in a way that is extreme and not balanced—in a way that may cause harm to ourselves and others. These emotions may also be correct.

So the intelligence button is one we need to press all the time particularly when we're angry, disgusted, feeling tormented, unhappy. Each of us, all mankind, and by mankind I mean every country, every nation, all of us, will solve our difficulty through our feelings of self-respect and regard for each other.

We have many groups of people who face daily the emotional outrage, the violence that consists of much of our daily lives. This difficulty we call violence is faced by people who realize the futility and the pain and suffering brought about by any sort of violence. Our police, our military do not think violence is a great sport. Our people, members of the clergy, psychiatrists, psychologists, social workers, people who assist with welfare are very aware of the daily tragedies they see or hear and it causes them great pain and discomfort.

As we go through life much of it is pleasant, so much satisfying and a lot of it seems as though we're in a cesspool, wading in it. We're in it. It's all around us but as we are aware of these difficulties and we struggle to leave this stench which clings to us while we are trying to be self-respectful and considerate of others—keep on going. Keep on going. We can go past the situation. We can clean ourselves off and we can enjoy this life.

Children—The Power and Authority of Parents

*A*gain with your permission...
This discussion is about children and parents: the necessary impression that the parent needs to give to the child about power and authority so the child may learn, hopefully by example, because the parents believe in individual meaning and significance. Not power and authority for its own sake.

These parents believe no one is more than them. No one is less than them and no one is the same as them. They attempt to give their child first and foremost confidence, and secondly the understanding that he is not to harm another. Through the child's awareness, practice and diligence, he or she gradually learns not to hit little Mary with the toy and not to stand on Johnny's toe. They learn that discomfort is not the way to live life— not to be on the receiving end and not to be pushing or annoying other people, young or old.

The parent fears, many times in an extreme way, because the child is liable to touch a hot stove, stand up on the chair or counter and lose their balance, possibly fall off—myriad fears that parents go through in attempting to keep the child from self-injury or injury by other children. This is the constant fear which can lead to some extremes in protecting the child. It can restrict the child at times. It can lessen the child's freedom, the child's opportunities to find out some things by themselves and this is done. We overprotect or we may protect with moderation so that the child does gain confidence—does gain and use its intellectual capacities to get along with other children.

What I believe occurs with a child is that many parents make the wrong moves with children through the rationale expressed as, "Well I love them so much I can't stand to see them hurt in any way." That's fine. That's well and good. Most people will agree and understand that but at the same time you need to let the children know this: "When you hurt yourself or suffer an injury what you are also doing is causing your parent indirectly to feel the pain, the intense pain of that injury."

The parent is feeling that pain much more intensely than the child is feeling it. The parent does not have the wound, the physical trauma but it has the intense pain of thinking this injury could have been worse. This injury may have been fatal or it may lead to the child's dying. I may lose this child. So the pain is personal to the parent in a greater way than it is to the child and it is very significant that the child understand. Not just a little, glib phrase when they are being spanked lightly or put into the corner to get their attention. You don't just say, "Well this hurts me more than it does you." This is very unsatisfying. It doesn't mean a thing and as far as the child is concerned, it's just a bunch of baloney. Sit down and tell the child, "When this happened to you, this little thing and you lost blood, the few drops," you tell the child, "in my head and in my mind and in my feelings, I have already felt I lost blood from that same injury and I don't have any mark on me. If this little bit of your blood caused you a lot of pain and it's a pretty big owie, you can see now my owie."

"So when you do something that is foolish or reckless that caused you injury, you must always consider that while you're doing it you just don't do this to you, you do it to your mother and father too. This is not just you expressing your individuality and freedom because at this moment you're really doing it to three people or more. So it means to be a bit more thoughtful when you make some moves. It doesn't mean you don't get on the horse. It doesn't mean you don't climb the tree. It doesn't mean you don't make an experiment but while you're doing it, take your brain along with your muscle. Remember Mommy and Daddy, and the pain; and you won't know all of what I'm saying until the day comes when you're a mommy or daddy. Then you'll understand all of what I'm trying to tell you now."

Unless this kind of conversation is initiated from a very early age—before children are two, before they get on their first pony, no matter what form it may take, the communication and the recognition has to be (and you need to put it into place) a two-way street, not just it's all coming from Mommy and Daddy. The child hasn't got yet this kind of accumulated knowledge, life experience, thoughts etc. Not yet. It's accumulating them but so far does not have the quantity and quality of friends, neighbors, interested parties. But the child needs to recognize that it also contributes to this mother/father team, brothers, sisters, friends, relatives and that what it does matters; even though it doesn't contribute much yet into the intellectual pot of ideas and considerations, plans, theories.

It does have the ability to attempt to understand and to attempt to respect and believe these parents, friends, and relatives even though the child does not quite understand what it is they are supposed to believe and why they are supposed to act in a particular way.The child eventually begins to grasp that it too is a part of the package here, that it isn't just having everything heaped on it—information, communication, ideas, manners, what you and what you don't do and all the no-no's. When you allow it by your expressions, your talk, and your examples the child then reflects back and says in effect to the interested party, "Yes, I am allowing you. I am trying to give you what you call permission. I want to understand and believe and I want to trust you and to see where and what direction you're attempting to give me."

A View
of Nature

With your helpful permission...
We look at nature and the ocean,
the mountains, the trees, animals, the
climate...we look at it, consider it every
day, talk about the weather much of the
time. We're very aware of it. When we're
out in the countryside, we're more
aware of it. And in our awareness—
down through the centuries to the
present—do we have any examples in
which nature and the things in nature
did something wrong? Did something
incorrect?

The fish in the ocean, some of
them go up the fresh water stream and
lay their eggs, the young hatch and the
life cycle of that fish, that particular
species will continue. We have the mi-
gration of reindeer, different animals,
birds, they go from here to there. We
even have volcanoes that explode at a

particular time after smoking for a while, making vague announcements that something's going to happen and we have earthquakes and we have tremors that occur. All these different things on earth occur so that life, nature may continue. May continue in balance.

Life continues. Everything grows. Everything lives. Everything perishes. Every thousand years roughly we have another inch of topsoil and nature goes on but does nature err? Does nature do anything wrong or incorrect? I don't believe so, yet mankind who is a part of nature, who is very involved with nature using the climate, the air, the water, the crops, the ocean, the fish, the forests for building materials, the mountains for stone and more building materials—mankind speaks often of right and wrong, correct and incorrect. We are taught a scientific explanation of the evolution of man. You know the one about the animal or whatever it's called crawling out of the water, groping up to become some kind of beast-like creature and gradually evolving to what it is today. It seems that the lower forms of animals appear to know what they are doing, while the highly evolved creature called man at times does not seem to know what he is doing or why he is doing it.

This seems odd. If mankind is of an evolutionary origin, it seems strange that we can err and make mistakes so often, particularly since the theory is we evolved from creatures, animals and man's brain evolved and now he has the greatest intelligence. It seems contradictory. It appears that he should make fewer mistakes, be even more in balance than the ordinary creatures of nature. And yet, is that what prevails? Do we say that mankind is in balance? With himself? With his fellow man? With his great intellect, his knowledge and his knowing he hasn't learned, he hasn't found out, and he doesn't seem to have the ability to get along and survive as well as a herd of cattle or a troop of baboons.

The benefits of the great mind and the great intellect are for what? Make a softer mattress? Invent ice cream? Concoct a variety of entertainments? We use our intelligence for many things which are beneficial to mankind and we use, or I would say, misuse our intelligence for many things which are not beneficial to mankind and which do not keep him in balance.

We speak today of the normal man. We imply the normal man is someone who is well balanced as it were. We use this word *normal* as a symbol, and we say of course no one like this really exists. What is it? We say *normal* is just an abstract consideration so that we can talk about individuals, groups of individuals. We set an arbitrary standard that we call normal. It seems to me that it's too bad that normalcy becomes something that really doesn't exist. We'd have to struggle to find an individual who scientists and scholars would all prove out—sifting as it were through people from many walks of life, find some being and say "Now this is the example of normalcy." Yet throughout nature, balance, normalcy, is there.

Nature is change. In any way when it appears to do something abnormal or incorrect, if we look at it in its entirety we see that mankind did some dredging here or cut down too many trees there, or tampered in some way with this remarkable balance, this remarkable achievement called nature—regardless again of its origin.

People sometimes imply that life is the result of a big explosion or is really a cosmic joke or it's all come about by chance, by accident. Well, by chance and accident nature continues. Balanced, capable and enduring...except when mankind interferes.

Mankind's capability and mankind's endurance and mankind's ability to continue is not looking so hot at the moment. We are doing a few things that are jeopardizing our life here on earth. But I believe that mankind through his divine connection will overcome his difficulties with the help and assistance of the constant awareness of his conscience and his true being.

The Individual

*A*nd yet again with your permission...

This series of comments is about
humanity but particularly the individual. And what happens and what
does he or she, young or old, go through
each day in the midst of this broad or
narrow spectrum called life.

Within just a twenty-four hour
period, a day and a night, we can wonder and consider why do we feel lonely.
Why do we feel bored and frustrated? I
believe boredom, frustration and loneliness, are not always negative feelings.
Many times in our boredom, our loneliness, and even in our frustrations we
may reflect, we may see, we may gain
insights and we may gain vision through
our continuous looking at what appears
to be the problem. "Why am I bored?

Why am I dull? Why am I lonely? Why am I frustrated? The rest of them are going on. They seem to be having a good time. They seem to be successful, satisfied for the most part and yet I go through this treadmill that, too many times, smacks of emptiness."

This happens with all of us. This isn't something that is given exclusively just for you. All of us know these things. All of us at one time or another question our sanity, question our beliefs. We say, "Well, this idea of God is a bunch of hokum, sophistry, something mankind has invented to help him out or possibly make him feel better in the midst of apparent chaos." We can say those things. We can think those things. We have an intelligence. We have an awareness. We have a reasonable mind. We have the ability to reflect. We have the ability to consider so when we're looking at things and wondering about thoughts and wondering about emptiness, I don't believe these feelings should be regarded as the result of God's punishment.

We need to have time, quiet time—it may be dull, it may be lonely. We need these times that allow us to

see ourselves and to see others with a
greater clarity. We really can't do that in
the midst of the hurly-burly, the activity,
the rapid movements of life: taking care
of the job, concentrating on our children,
raising our family, thinking about our
loved ones, our friends, our marriage, all
of those things require much attention,
much of our time and the majority of our
efforts. So our quiet times are not times
really of punishment. They are times
that allow us to reaffirm, re-establish, to
make progress I would say, to grow, to
expand even though it seems like we've
been on a treadmill, a mental treadmill,
thinking about and talking about the
same things over and over and over
again and the changes seem so minute
that you don't remember what you
thought about last year although we
know it was related to our loneliness
and boredom and our consideration of
punishment.

We have all these feelings and
these confusions which give us what we
call stress. All of what we may know and
learn is still based upon the clarity and
the simplicity and the courage, the
beauty and the harmony implicit in that
declaration of the wise teachers, "Do

unto others as you would have them do unto you." We need to have a feeling of self-respect before we can show others respect. We need to have a feeling of love.

Love is not earned, love is allowed. Love is permitted. Love is accepted or love is ignored. But unless we have a feeling of self-respect, a strong feeling of self-respect it is very difficult for us to understand and appreciate and utilize the golden rule.

We need to see and appreciate and know that God our Creator, Allah, the Great Spirit—however He's termed—does not have favorites. We are all Her favorites.

So when we consider again our loneliness, discomfort, frustration, stress and all that, we know that all His children have this at different times, different occasions. It may appear to us that we've got more than someone else and, of course, the person who has all the money and all the fame and all the applause, they must be wonderful and we must be less. This is really another way of ignoring His love.

Do not temper or moderate it: You are everything, you are to Him everything. You are His happiness, Her joy.

Form Change

With your permission, always with your permission, I want to consider for a moment what an infant is prior to birth, eight months, eight and a half months in age. If that infant can hear the mother speak aloud, it has ears, can it hear others who may be in the company of the mother? Maybe. When the infant is born, is the infant thrilled and does the infant appear to be enjoying this situation that we call birth or does it appear angry, resentful, uncomfortable, put out as it were, from this comfortable, satisfying place where it was within its mother?

We consider birth to be a blessed event, we who are spectators as it were, the audience. But I wonder if the infant regards it as a particularly splendid occurrence. As we go through life and we are all eventually faced with the idea of dying, changing form from this form that we have, this physical body, and our thoughts, everything that we have that expresses our individual self or psyche, ego, our soul, our essence, whatever. As we go through life and we may consider on occasion that we won't be around forever, in this form at least, so we may use a phrase, instead of talking about death, dying: changing form.

Now when we were born, everything seemed to work out all right no matter how unpleasant it seemed. And there are many of us who regard changing form, dying as a finality. That's it. Okay. That's what you believe. Fine. But we can consider other notions. If it's okay to believe that it's a finality, it's also okay to believe that it isn't a finality. It appears to be and yet we were born without much control of the situation. This may occur also when we change form.

Now when we were aware of life—whatever that awareness may consist of (I'm speaking now of the infant) everything for the most part turned out all right. Now as we approach another dramatic change, there may be different mental and emotional equipment that we can't understand or describe as yet. And because we cannot visualize it (any more than an infant could visualize what was occurring at birth, except for being aware that it wasn't too fond of the idea), when we are all faced with an unknown situation, it certainly gets our attention and is frightening. It is disturbing to say the least.

But we did all right the first time. We did all right. In this form we knew beauty, we knew joy, we knew satisfactions, we knew what grief was and we knew what unpleasantness can be but for the most part we were aware of pleasure, enjoyment, love, comfort. We knew what all these things were and we wanted more of the same.

All the perfection and beauty that was placed on this earth—things that we observe, that we're aware of—are very reassuring that life does have a continuity. We see it all around us - nature, climate, universe. And I consider and others consider that we have been given everything that was necessary to live, prior to birth. And when we change form perhaps we will have another, different, unusual but satisfying birth.

Hope

(Note: The following essay is an excerpt from the author's book ANOTHER PARADISE, published in 1987.)

This essay is not saying everything in the 'good old days' was wonderful. There was more than enough grief even in those different days. - T.L.

Mankind seems to have lost his sense of drive, feeling, and opportunity to fear and hopelessness.

In the thirties and forties, the morality of the neighborhood existed. Crime was at a low ebb in spite of the Depression, in spite of the economic needs. I say low ebb in relationship to what's going on and has been going for the past recent years.

Large companies did not move people all over the United States. People were usually working for a company and worked for the company all their working lives. It was the usual thing to do. They lived in the same place among the same people. Morality was strong and meaningful. They believed in God because God delivered, did what He said: God took care of His own. A man worked to support his family, saw to it that his kids got off to the best possible start he could give them and he lived in the hope that his children would do better than he had—economically better. He did not consider that it was a need that his children do better than he or his wife morally. The hope was for economic improvement, security.

The Depression was frightening. Approximately one out of four people was without jobs. But the three who had jobs sustained our country. The one without the job could look at the three with jobs and have hope that he one day too would have a job. The job was vital, not particularly the pay—and the fact of having a job held promise and the opportunity existed to advance through going to school nights, or doing good quality work; or doing more work and in so doing getting promoted and earning a bigger paycheck.

Mankind at this time had a sense of assurance in spite of staring at World War II and in spite of the Depression. The young at this time did not feel that their parents were fools, and that life was empty and that God was a mistake or sick. They believed that they could do better. They had hope in spite of the Depression, in spite of World War II. The parents were not filled with guilt. They did not feel that they were doing their children a disservice by rearing them, by bringing them into the world.

The neighborhoods in which they lived and worked for the most part were peaceful. Despite the class of neighborhood—lower, upper or whatever— the people felt secure in their lives. They had a naiveté. They had a belief in goodness, fairness, justice, law and order, mother and father, church, education—all the traditional institutions now called the establishment. These institutions did not fail them. Government did provide a means for coping with the Depression. Government did successfully manage to win a military victory in World War II. People had hope. People could see, believe. People could see others who had it made. What I mean by having it made is that they thought that life was not just a collection of status symbols. It was a belief that if they did well, that if their children did well, that their children's children would do better. They saw it as an ongoing movement towards more security, a better civilization, peace, and a strong sense of hope. Today, I believe this has all changed. Today I cannot conceive of anyone who can say they have it made. The fear of the bomb hangs over anyone from the poorest to the wealthiest. Our civilization as we know it can disappear. Our civilization now is apparent in its degeneracy through the widespread use of harmful drugs and suffering constant symptoms of terminal illnesses—apparently in grave danger because of the bomb and doubt that solutions exist to the bomb threat. I believe one of the most alarming symptoms of this degeneracy is that people are losing their sense of hope. They do not think, they do not believe that their children's children will live except in scattered instances—survivors of the nuclear blast living like animals, starting over again as it were with a smaller earth, an earth that has less of the beauty and less of the means of survival: agriculture, hunting and fishing and the like. I think this is considered by most people of today—not talked about but deep within each individual the fear is dominant that they will not see their children's children. They will not even consider that though they may be dead that their great grandchildren will survive and live as they did prior to the atom bomb.

Prior to the atom bomb and drug culture it seemed possible to have it made. It was possible that life was worthwhile. It was possible to have a feeling of immortality you'd see in future generations of your own. To strive and succeed. Economically and socially become more civilzed. By civilized I mean a lessening of famines, a lessening of man's inhumanity to man, a lessening of economic stress, a lessening of any kind of warfare, a lessening of man being frightened by his fellow man.

We realized at the time of the Great Depression and World War II that a mother and father were necessary to raise most children who were not neurotic and who were not confused in society, who did not have to resort to constant distractions in order to escape the fears that have developed since the discovery, the use, the knowledge of the atom bomb.

It seems that most children today

do not have goals, a sense of anything ongoing. They cannot develop a sense of anything ongoing. They cannot develop a sense of hope when faced with the constant threat of worldwide annihilation. Mankind has lost much of his faith in God. We've had all kinds of changes, changes for the sake of change, not for betterment. Within some of our oldest religions we find changes— Catholicism appears to be declining. Protestantism also has a lower attendance.

People of today feel lost. The consequences are dope and guilt from an early age, anything for a comforting distraction. Science fiction is admired because perhaps we can all get into a space ship and disappear from this fear, from this planet and start anew without the thought of war. People want to go back to nature. That means in all the trappings of civilization everything technological will disappear and we'll go back to the age when there was more peace and security than what we think of today. We do not think of living from day to day and enjoying life: the beauty and the grandeur, the thrill that life is. We look upon it today as, can we survive? Can we get by for another week, another month, another year to buy more things, enjoy more things because the money is becoming valueless, our lives are becoming valueless?

Let's get all the admiration and the acclaim that we can cram into a few short years, a few short months, a few short weeks. Let's do it now because there is no future. There is nothing for us. We fear and suffer guilt. Our children say to us, "You have given us a living death. We take dope because we have to. We're filthy, we're degenerate. We're immoral because there's nothing else for us and why should we listen to you, our parents, when you've brought the world and the earth to this despicable, empty consideration that we attempt to call life. You did this, Mother and Father. You did this to us. You did not love us. You hate us." Don't trust anyone over thirty.

The parents seem to have no answers so the parents cannot discipline, the parents cannot control. The children run amok. The parents wring their hands. The courts are full. The jails are full. Our hearts are empty.

We do not see that life can still be meaningful. We have given up. We do not work with our children. We do not strive. We are overwhelmed.

The degeneracy of our civilization in the United States is a form of giving up. We do not know any more what it means to have it made. We have no sureness. We have only questions, no answers. We have doubts. Our belief in God is minimized because what can God do about it—to solve this problem—and if He can do something about it, why isn't He doing it?

So we consider an afterlife. Spiritualism is very much in vogue. Life after death is extremely popular. Not in the old-fashioned religious way but with the idea that has now become socially acceptable to believe in a life cycle where we become different persons—that we've led lives in the past. Perhaps we have but we are looking at it as a form of escape. We're not looking at it as something that we need to do something about.

We are not attempting to solve the problem. We believe, perhaps, that it is better to give up to someone more powerful or someone threatening so we do not have war. You know the brilliant saying, "Better Red than dead." People would submit themselves and future generations to a type of slavery just so we could all live as though that would be some guarantee. The emptiness is appalling.

Our thinking is blinding us. We need to consider that there are answers. There are solutions. We do not have to submit to our self-tyranny which is constantly refueled by the sense of guilt. We cannot move onward, cannot move into a more civilized attitude through fear. We can only move when we consider that our thinking needs be rational and pragmatic and we must dominate our fear, we must dominate that intense emotion through our intellect.

Now is the time for people to think, to consider, and to want to strive to see once again that we can have it made.

Luxury

With your permission, we may consider enjoying luxury if we are all able to eat first.

We all work. Those of us who have jobs, those of us who need jobs, we work. We work at getting a job. But why do we work? We work so we can pay our bills, so we can eat, have a place to live, have clothing to wear, take care of our children. But mainly when we have these things done, and these basic things accomplished, we work for leisure time so we can watch the games on TV, take our family on vacation, go fishing, go bowling, golfing, swimming, whatever. This is what we do with our time off, with our leisure.

Whether we're aware of it or not, most of us have today in our civilized world the greatest luxury and the greatest ease that mankind has attained so far. To enjoy what we have we need our homes, our apartments, our cabins, our house trailers, whatever we live in, even our tents—we need to maintain that environment as we would our vast natural environment. We need in our homes neatness, cleanliness,and beauty. A can of paint doesn't cost a lot and your home can be painted any color that appeals to you.

In your home, without great expense you can have beautiful pictures—pictures you enjoy, reproductions of priceless masterpieces for a few dollars. These things are not expensive. You can have great music, copies of art objects. If you can't see from your windows, trees, sea or rivers, you can have plants, beautiful plants. If you can't have plants you can have a window box. Put some seeds in it, grow some flowers. You can have natural beauty no matter how humble or inexpensive your dwelling may be.You have the means of living without great wealth, of living as comfortably as the person with great wealth, because we have electricity.

We live better today even in an

ordinary way than kings or monarchs or pharaohs lived in the past with their tremendous wealth, with their tremendous hordes of people attending them. We have a luxurious style of living and we don't recognize it. We say, "Well our dwellings, our cars, what we really have is not good enough." All right. Fine. It isn't good enough. It isn't enough. You have goals and you wish to achieve a nicer home, better cars; fine, do it. But don't forget while you're doing it that you have a wonderful way of living. No matter how plain it may be. Of course you compare it with how multi-millionaires or billionaires live. We say, "Oh boy. This isn't so hot." Oh yes it is. You don't have to lack for a lot of beauty in this life and it doesn't require a great deal of money to have comfortable, pleasant, and enjoyable surroundings. This can be done if you want it.

You can only wear one outfit at a time and eat three meals a day, millionaire or not. We enjoy life no matter our income—no matter that the grass looks greener on the other side of the fence—when you realize that the happiest people, the people who are the most content are those who use their leisure, their time off, to think, to reflect, to listen to music, read books, look at their beautiful pictures; enjoy fishing, sports, plays, films, the company of other people and conversations with them. When we put our leisure time to this kind of use we can see that these are the things that enable us to be happy, content. When we are always looking, always wanting—this is okay. That's fine. But while we're looking and wanting and desiring more don't ignore, don't forget, don't overlook what you have. You really have, we all really have a very wonderful way today of living. Luxuriously.

Appendix

Variations of the Golden Rule

<u>List One</u>
Source: Stevenson, Burton.
The Home Book of Quotations.
Ninth Edition. New York:
Dodd, Mead, and Co.,
1958.

Is there one word which may serve as a
rule of practice for all one's life? The
master said, Is not *reciprocity* such a
word? What you do not want done to
yourself, do not do to others.
> Confucius, *Analects,* Bk. XV, Ch. 23

True goodness springs from a man's own
heart. All men are born good.
> Confucius, *Analects,* (Giles, tr.)

Every man takes care that his neighbor
does not cheat him. But a day comes when
he begins to take care that he does not
cheat his neighbor. Then all goes well.
> Emerson, *Conduct of life:* Worship

Therefore if anyone would take these two words to heart and use them for his own guidance, he will be almost without sin. These two words are *bear* and *forbear*.

> Epictetus, (Aulus Gellius, *Noctes Atticae,* Bk XVII, Ch. 19, Sec. 6)

The Golden Law,
"do as ye would be done by."

> Robert Godfrey, *Physics* (1674)

Thence arises that Golden Rule of dealing with others as we would have others deal with us.

> Isaac Watts, *Logick,* (1725)

Look to be treated by others as you have treated others.

> Publilius Syrus, *Sententiae,* No. 1

You must expect to be treated by others as you yourself have treated them.

> Seneca, *Epistulae ad Lucilium,* Epis. XCIV, Sec. 43. Quoted.

<u>List Two</u>
Source: Mencken, H.L.
*A New Dictionary of Quotations on
Historical Principles.* New York: Alfred A.
Knopf, 1960

Do not do to others what would anger you
if done to you by others.
Ascribed to Isocrates, c. 375 B.C.

What thou thyself hatest, do to no man.
Tobit IV, 14,c.180 B.C.

The question was once put to Aristotle
how we ought to behave to our friends;
and his answer was, "As we should wish
them to behave to us."
Diogenes Laertius: *Lives of the
Philosophers,* c. 150 B.C.

This is the sum of all true righteousness:
deal with others as thou wouldst thyself
be dealt by. Do nothing to thy neighbor
which thou wouldst not have him do to
thee hereafter.
The Mahabharata, c. 150 B.C.

Whatsoever thou wouldst that men should not do to thee, do not do that to them. This is the whole Law. The rest is only explanation.

>Hillel Ha-Babli: *The Sabbath,*XXXI, c. 30 B.C.

All things whatsoever ye would that men should do to you, do ye even so to them: for this is the law and the prophets.

>*Matthew VII, 12,* c. 75

As ye would that men should do to you, do ye also to them likewise.

>*Luke, VI, 31,* c. 75

What thou avoidest suffering thyself seek not to impose on others.

>Epictetus: *Encheiridion,* c. 100

Whatsoever ye do not wish should be done unto you, do not do to others.

>*Acts XV, 29* c. 875

All things whatsoever that thou wouldst not wish to be done to thee, do thou also not to another.

>*The Didache, or Teaching of the Twelve Apostles,* c. 135

Whatever the Christians do not wish to be
done to them they do not do to another.
St. Aristides: *Apology for the
Christian Faith, XV* c. 160

As ye will that men do to you, and do ye to
them in like manner.
John Wyclif: *Tr. of Luke VI,* 31,1389

Do as ye wald be done to.
David Fergusson: *Scottish
Proverbs,* 1641

Whatsoever you require that others
should do to you, that do ye to them.
Thomas Hobbes: *Leviathan,* I, 1651

My duty towards my neighbor is to love
him as myself, and to all men as I would
they should do unto me.
*The Book of Common Prayer
(Catechism),* 1662

The evil which you do not wish done to
you, you ought to refrain from doing to
another, so far as may be done without
injury to some third person.
Henry More: *Encheiridion ethicum,*
IV, 1667

Desire nothing for yourself which you do not desire for others.

Baruch Spinoza: *Ethica IV,* 1677

If the prisoner should ask the judge whether he would be content to be hanged, were he in his case, he would answer no. Then, says the prisoner, do as you would be done to.

John Selden: *Table-Talk,* 1689

Should that most unshaken rule of morality, and foundation of all social virtue, "that one should do as he would be done unto," be proposed to one who never heard of it before, but yet is of capacity to understand its meaning, might he not without any absurdity ask a reason why?

John Locke: *Essay Concerning Human Understanding, I,* 1690

Be you to others kind and true,
     As you'd have others be to you,
And neither do nor say to men
     Whate'er you would not take again.

Isaac Watts: *Divine Songs of Children,* pref., 1715

Do as you would be done by, is the surest method of pleasing.

> Lord Chesterfield: *Letter to his son,*
> Oct. 16, 1747

To do as you would be done by, is the plain, sure, undisputed rule of morality and justice.

> Lord Chesterfield: *Letter to his son,*
> Sept.27, 1748

No man doth think others will be better to him that he is to them.

> Benjamin Whichcote: *Moral and Religious Aphorisms,* 1753

I must always act in such a way that I can at the same time will that the maxim by which I act should become a universal law.

> Immanuel Kant: *Grundlegung Zur Metaphysic der Sitten,* I, 1785

We ought to act that part towards another which we would judge to be right in him to act toward us, if we were in his circumstances and he in ours.

> Thomas Reid: *Essays on the Active Powers,* V, 1788

The duty of man ... is plain and simple,
and consists of but two points: his duty to
God, which every man must feel, and
with respect to his neighbor, to do as he
would be done by.

> Thomas Paine: *The Rights of Man,*
> I, 1791

To do, as one would be done by, and to
love one's neighbor as one's self,
constitute the ideal perfection of
utilitarian morality.

> J. S Mill: *Utilitarianism,* II, 1863

Our conscience teaches us it is right, our
reason teaches us it is useful, that men
should live according to the Golden Rule.

> W. Winwood Reade: *The Martrydom
> of Man,* III, 1872

Reason shows me that if my happiness is
desirable and a good, the equal happiness
of any person must be equally desirable.

> Henry Sidgwick: *The Methods of
> Ethics,* III, 1874

Do unto others as you would have others
do unto you in like case.

> P.A. Kropotkin: *La morale
> anarchiste,* 1891

Do as you would be done by.
      English Proverb,
      based on *Matthew VII,* 12 c. 75

When we and ours have it in our power
to do for you and yours what you and
yours have done for us and ours, then
we and ours will do for you and yours
what you and yours have done for us
and ours.
      - Old English Toast

Order Form

With your permission, we will ship you *The "Keep on Going" Spirit* by priority mail.

Send your request to:
> **Keep Going Publishers**
> **Box 545**
> **Kettle Falls, Washington 99141**

No. of copies	Price	Total
	$14.95	
	Tax	
	Shipping	
	Total	

Tax: add 7.5% for books sent to Washington addresses.

Shipping: $4.00 for the first book and $2.00 for each additional book.
Please enclose a check or money order for the above amount.

The author is available for presentations on money, business, and ethics to groups and associations. Please inquire at the above address.

Please ship to:
Name:_____
Address:_____
City:_____State:____Zip:_____

───── *Order Form* ─────

With your permission, we will ship you *The "Keep on Going" Spirit* by priority mail.

Send your request to:
Keep Going Publishers
Box 545
Kettle Falls, Washington 99141

No. of copies	Price	Total
	$14.95	
	Tax	
	Shipping	
	Total	

Tax: add 7.5% for books sent to Washington addresses.

Shipping: $4.00 for the first book and $2.00 for each additional book.
Please enclose a check or money order for the above amount.

> *The author is available for presentations on money, business, and ethics to groups and associations. Please inquire at the above address.*

Please ship to:
Name:_____
Address:_____
City:_____ State:_____ Zip:_____